MUSES

To Vincent

MUSES

DAVID HATHWELL

David Hathwell

David Robert Books

Published by David Robert Books
PO Box 541106
Cincinnati, OH 45254-1106

ISBN: 9781625491992

Poetry Editor: Kevin Walzer
Business Editor: Lori Jareo

Author photo: Carl Hathwell

Cover and book design: Jan Camp
ArcLightBooks.com/Hathwell

Publicity photo of Fred Astaire and Rita Hayworth for *You Were Never Lovelier:* Columbia Pictures, 1942 (public domain)

for Helen Cunningham,
good critic and good friend

CONTENTS

Call to the Reader

The Need for Echoes

Not the canyon kind. Never those—
nature's cunning parlor trick
wherein the Maestro, all in black,
inviting exclamations from the guests,

severs—Presto!—sound from sense,
conjuring a rush of shuffled sound
that, reducing as it multiplies,

answers all our efforts to express
with a resounding *less.*

Not those, no—
rather gestures of affirmation, of assent,
the seconding reply—the nod, the *yes*—
that grants our inmost notion
—Ecco!—outward being, embodiment,

lends shadow substance, confers
upon the homeless sense of self
the sensation of a dwelling place,

and distances awhile the awful boom
of echoes of the other kind.

MUSES

Orchestra, Advanced

Safe passage to character and culture
only to them, our dreaming elders.
For us, the wandering young,
fifty minutes' reprieve guaranteed
(attendance required) from the day's
grim drills of ordered aimlessness,
the weight of unsafe silences.

Having no eye for elevation,
we watched the score before us
and now and then the wagging wand
beyond, counted as we tapped out beats,
marking time until our coded cue—
then struck, bowed, plucked, or blew.
How good to be an oboe once a day.

In those rising exclamations above all,
where, from heightened watchfulness,
we looked to the truth of rhythm and
pitch, touch and timbre to mute
distinction, level difference—find
our voices in the massing sound,
knowing when to speak and how.

When Musicians Applaud

When musicians applaud, they do the oddest thing.
To praise the command of the maestro,
Or the skill of another member of the ranks,
These masters of music and decorum—
Masters of movement in time—
Abandon all art to pound their feet
Against the soundboard of the stage.

Nothing civil now. Close by—in the next hall—
A band of rebels tramples the palace floor,
Mouths mute for stealth, weapons raised;
Or farther off, in the shadows of a forest haunt,
The gathered pack beats bark, drum, and gourd
To celebrate the kill—no rise to a climax
Then decrescendo, no easing to a cadence,
Just explosive start and stop.

It must be that they still are as they were,
Before melody was added, and room for silence,
And the power found in the single beat
To marshal breath and muscle, joint and limb
In the making of a long, shaped, concerted sound.

Recalled to their task, the forces rally now—
Hang poised within their ranks until, at the signal
From the leader, they raise their instruments again
And together celebrate beauty.

Fred's Girl

Astaire's partners are never anywhere as good. But sometimes better.

—Jeff Escoffier, dance writer, in conversation

Truant Muse master, would-be mortal,
Apollo on his strolling visit fumbled
his disguise—the old, ageless rubber mask
and high extraplanetary chic ("Astaire"!),
sleeves to gloves, slacks to pumps
to hide the lineaments of deity;
the sprung displays of purest energy
neither gathered nor renewed,
in succeeding gestures earthward—
blasts of rat-tat tapping syncopation—
or released into the air without the weight
of gravity, each crowned and brightly
finished, all rounded and complete;
then the signs by which we mortals
know him best: radiance, serenity.

But Ginger, Joan, Rita, Paulette—
creatures of flesh no doubt. Standing,
at first, coltishly uncertain, in time
coaxed forward by the master to try
her untried limbs, each submits her being
to test on test of line and balance—
bends and dips, easy turns then whipped
and spun, leaps and prancing shuffles,

struts urged to gallops, lunges held,
reversed, at full, half, double speed.

Blood racing—breathless, gleaming—
she dances with her own, ideal image,
but he, with godly gallantry, bids us
watch the girl, *delight in her,* shows us
not their distance but her unlikely brave
advances, her thrilling proximity.

Flesh so near to spirit, she exults.
In her joy she wants to laugh, exclaim,
but the momentum of these movements
has her, pulls her, lifts her onward, up.
This is close to heaven—what could
ever be as good? She's Fred's girl,
she's in heaven, she can hardly speak.

Red Dress

Two gold bands,
nestled matrimonially
against a soft blue field,
offer the fine symmetry
of twinned circles burnished
to an even glow. The page
frames them brilliantly—
reachably distant and still—
for the admiring eye.

Elsewhere, emerging from
an evening crowd, a lovely dress—
luxe geometries of line and
curve alive in movement,
its rich red many reds—
gathers light and lifts from the page.
Its ruby radiance fills to the brim—
fills to overflowing and fills and fills.
It becomes Red Dress, wins all
red dresses to its glorious form—
the only one and all you need.

Poplar

Surely this one is meant for our delight—
When, hidden in the green, a hundred butterflies,
Catching a breeze, flutter sage and silver wings
In tethered flight—or a dozen veiled limbs,
Lifting in the wind, swing their lavish weave
Of flashing bangle, leaf, and twig coyly
In and out of sight.

Hard, that is, to see within the lovely show
Economies of growth, accommodated
Circumstance—to recognize the play of leaf
And branch, the rich invention of their repertoire,
As strategies devised by chance to ease
The take of air and light.

For pleasure freely taken, all due thanks—
Applaud the accidental show. All honor
To the spectacle—clearest to the nourished eye—
Of gratifying need: the appetite for abundance,
The will to sense and feed.

The Pigeon Is a Shoe

Artful decoy at the curb,
working its spell from forty feet—
a straight-line pull across the pavement,
gait steadied by stony resignation, eyes forward.

And the pigeon is only a shoe.
Really an ankle boot, I see, the neck
folded to the toe. The leather slumps,
a dead white worn to gray along the body.

So I'm spared the memory of a bird—
on this corner, at this hour,
with or without visible injury—
and, too close, the stark look of afterlife.

Though here comes a cat from months ago,
on its side on a hearth at Guerrero
and Fourteenth, here it is among the bins,
a calico stretched out lazily in the early afternoon,
its mouth open, baring the smallest teeth,
and a split pomegranate at the neck.

During Restless Sleep a Scene of Remarkable Stillness

On the far side of a river,
holly lines the riverbank.
The leaves are lacquered tiles.

In the distance, along the horizon,
giant cypresses, all indigo, link
their lower limbs.

Between, a field of grass
rolls unbroken
in suspended waves.

The pond, or lake—too still
to be a river—is a better blue
than the unmarked sky.

Within its deep painterly glow
the holly hangs in amethyst clusters,
and it brims.

Nothing moves. No breeze
touches a branch or leaf
or plays over the meadow.

Lake, brush, grass, and trees
hold their line and color
under the sun's probing light.

Nothing stirs in the hidden depths
to make the water ripple, or spill
beyond its borders into the land.

Reading the Fall

for my students

Watching and watching the water fall—
The wild roaring plunge chased by light—
In minutes my eyes, tired by the commotion
Of so much change and sameness, climbed up
The fall to the quieter motion at the head—

From below, just a sunken lower jaw
Edged with teeth of stones, some smoothed,
Most still cracked and angled, and spewing,
Where stone met stone or from hidden facets,
Streams and splashes into the widening fall.

A splash curled and plunged; I saw it fall,
Fall and fall in heavier, headlong slow motion—
Grand effect, I supposed, of the claim on sight
Of its single downward-glittering arc.
Senses quickening for a deeper vision—

Eyes again at the mouth—I caught this splash
And that and that, reaching to hold in view
Their separate, slowed descents. Reached
And failed. Though before the blur: a glimpse into
The sources of grandeur, the falls within the fall.

* * *

The many in the one says the divining mystic,
The seer. But I am nothing of those; I am a reader,

Called by chance to read, in a privileged glimpse
Beyond the wash of first impressionism,
The hidden power of words within the word.

For watchful eyes, signal gestures—little phrases
For sounds, sights—form and mingle, each joining
The gathering force of its sure, coursing progress
To a grander spectacle of fulfillment, its cadences,
Final yet reverberant, the cadences of majesty.

Now I heard, in the roaring fall, Caddie's
Then Luster's then Dilsey's "Hush!"—saw
Willy plunge, at last, into the peaceful dark.
The bleak tidal ruckus of the bight brings
To shore its happy riot of correspondences,

Stella for falling star repeats for good
Blanche's deep descent, stone extrudes once more
To thrust the friends apart, and, borne back
On an implacable current, Gatsby reaches still
Toward flowering white-green wonder.

Song

I'm five-seven or five-eight
Depending on the day.
Mood can do that.

Sometimes I wake up
Billy Collins and the
Words seem to flow.

To shape the flow
I'm a riverbank, a weir,
The wind, the moon.

I'm a river, a sea god—
Jealous waterlord, shape
Shifter, caster of spells.

I rage against insurgents
Until, subdued, they sing
My sovereignty.

When the song is right
I'm muscled and lean
And have turnout.

I rise from my desk,
Majestic, and I dance.
Oh how I dance.

Sure Thing

You're a brick,
Yes, a hard red block that you can trust,
Unless it's accidentally cracked
Or whacked to dust.

Or rather you're a diamond,
Superbly tough and brilliant once it's ground,
Providing it's been mined
And found.

No—you're an elixir,
Whose wholesome powers to restore and mend
Magically arrest decline
Until the end.

And I'm a voice
That tells you what you always surely knew:
That language is prepared to lie
When you ask it to.

Sunday Sorrow

The piercing edge
is loss, the end
bearing down
or about to.

Home in failing
light, punctual
as the hour.
But sometimes
the early
exigent guest.

For me now
it flashes in
early morning
sightings of
the slippery
dead,

someone in
the lasting
stillness, an
old aroma,
the curve of
a spoon,

in the oak
of the kitchen
table Mother
or an aunt,

looking back
toward five
o'clock, dawn
or dusk in
her eyes,
waving or
pointing.

Tropes

The death of death.
How fine a trope.
In a thimble
All of Christian hope.

Is it Donne's?
In wit and moment, yes,
If not in word.
He wields it best.

Show thy sting!
Armed to face a foe—
Man or thing—
Now we stand to win.

But how if death
Refuses being—
Declines the role—
Fulfilled instead
In nothingness?

Time to put the play
Of words to work
To furnish absence—
Frame the simple end—
The very death—of death.

We'll begin again.
Commemorate the dead.
Take flower, candle, song—
All that might be sung
Or said—into empty rooms.

Voices

When I see my hand
and see my mother's hand
I hear her voice,

not words, though
she is speaking slowly,
or quietly singing,
a song half remembered
or a song of her own,

an almost-speech,
soft and finely textured
as the skin of my hand,
that lifts to a tremolo,
an easy fluttering,
of secret delight or
longing or grief,
then, wavering, fades
to a low reedy hum,

lifts and falls until, caught
by the spell of its song,
I can believe that it beckons,
that its message is for me.

Family Stories

i. m. Crecensio (1888?–1964)

Retelling his story brings
a sense of permanence.
The past isn't finished.
It's still here. Listen . . .

So she tells the story again,
to the same ears if need be,
tells it again until, in time,
by the power of the telling,

a young man named for a dead uncle
and lost in a northern land
gives way to the father,
striding visionary,

until duty yields to devotion,
doubt to bright resolve,
and the hard, broken turf
of hunch and happenstance

to open road and crossroad,
whose travel traces, at last,
the well-told tale's rise and fall,
its timeless symmetries.

This Week's China

Aunt Renée was expert in betrayal.
Uncle Jack stood up and swore I do
and then before you knew it
left her holding a full-grown baby
and a fat monthly debt.
But she lived and learned and life went on
until Uncle Henry—her own personal savior
and Judas all in one *ha ha*—
did just about the same—the prince
who called himself a family man
and said it was her turn now to feel like royalty.

So that settled any doubt.
Uncle Jack and Uncle Henry became
twin King Tuts in a private museum
that practically built itself—portable,
secure yet open all hours for guided tours
featuring the two old standbys
but, first, items recently acquired:
this unkept date, that unappreciated sandwich,
this unanswered prayer or phone call
(*Lean in close to take in the detail*),
that unreturned handbag, smile, friendship.

Back at the entrance, where it was time
to be reminded of the precise value
of the show, Aunt Renée's eyes—
sharp and searching then—seemed

to direct its meaning straight at me:
Look how easily a promise made
is broken—even if it's forged in steel.
Then a shrug of the shoulders and brows
to punctuate futility, and bitter final words
I loved (and silently said with her):
This week's china! . . .

Toward the end the museum closed.
On short notice Aunt Renée retired
behind grudging speech, and a blank gaze
that leveled everything before it—
us, the changing sky, rooms ever smaller,
those graying tiles and fluorescent lights—
and frightened everyone but me.

Aunt Renée, I thought, had liquidated
all her holdings, exchanged them
for a kind of song, sustaining, sounding
just for her, the music, played and shuffled
and played again, of the sudden shattering
of a bowl, the crash of bursting glass,
the rude bang of a blowout, the ripping
of a sleeve on a latch, the soft splintering
of ice beneath the feet, and—if she's lucky
(Peace be with you, Aunt Renée!)—
the bright clanging of a pearly gate.

somehow installed, in the hot light
of an August afternoon
while the lazy dozed,
in the middle of her own backyard.

She imagined nubbly creatures
joined by curling filaments,
piping in their alien language
the excitement of the mission—

whose purpose she was fated
not to know. Before her eyes
the lily landed silently again,
backwards—rose a yard or so,

hovered (a dainty lampshade?),
revved to a whirling spin,
then leapt lightly skyward,
traceless in the grass and gravel.

Again master of her world,
she turned and padded off,
cup in hand, to check the wash.
It was all up to her.

She had her anecdote,
and would wield her ready words
to hold their ears and dumb, rapt faces
until they believed it.

Through My Window

If we had a keen vision and feeling of all ordinary
human life . . .

—George Eliot, *Middlemarch*

Behind the spare proscenium of the frame
a woman enters, stage right, on a beeline to stage left.
Groomed for business, striding eyes forward,
she cannot see, as she swerves to miss,
the young man just appearing upstage center,
through the double doors of a café storefront
not, I recall, a scrim.

His sight trained equally on what lies ahead,
he hauls a strip of rubber flooring, hiked
against a hip, slowly downstage center
to his station at the curb, then takes a beat,
and drops it flush along the ledge.
Standing straight (not so young, I see),
in his clean white apron of the day,
he seems to me, as he inspects the mat
to weigh the task, to eye within its length
the prospect of the day's familiar labors
yet to come, and, as he turns to make his way
upstage and off, to trudge, with lowered sight,
a narrowed, beaten track that, truth to tell,
I'm pleased to be unable to pursue.

Stage empty, vision idling, my mind
is freed to contemplate the frame.
If all the world's a stage, who, I muse,
must be its privileged spectators?
And I start the tale of a minor Roman god,
or better still a legendary ancient king,
a king, let's say, of former Thessaly,
who, covetous of higher-powered sight,
tries to scale Olympus for the view
and then is punished for his crime,
with the gift of perfect vision
and, high upon a promontory, everlasting life.

I see, in a head bent back and away against an infinite sky,
a pair of restless wild eyes locked in striving not to see,
and hear, through the tortured mouth that crowns him now,
the long, unrelieving cries of boundless all-seeing impotence . . .

Saved from griefs so unlike my own,
I cozy back to figures on a well-framed stage
—at the moment three, poised, it seems,
on an apron for a bow, but with profiled heads,
on craned necks, turned smartly to stage left—
toward, I see, a late commuting bus looming
as if cued. Heaving dutifully under its load,
it drags to a dead stop dead center, in time
revives, and—neat little vanishing act to give
the scene a close—lumbers off an emptied stage
to only God knows where.

Finding Myself in the Morning

The unstoppable wellspring is still.
From the next room a heaving and settling
too removed by sleep and silence
to summon, yet, his lifelong companion.

In minutes memory will seep through,
find its way in along old channels,
in its deepest reaches gather to a flow,
the past a second bloodstream pumping
into the present, speeding the pulse,
flushing the skin: his companion again,
their brother, her friend . . .

For now, I can sit alone at this table,
in this cool bright air, and trace
with slow fingers these dark veins
ambered in oak. I can hear faraway traffic
and, below, a clack of heels and silence
and something like a shout, and not wonder
who is speaking, or what comes next.

Parting Word

Finishing

The love of form is a love of endings.
—Louise Glück, "Celestial Music"

What if it's somehow like the end
of a good, a well-told story?
Then you'll have completion,
have, better still, *completeness.*

The reckoning will be a rounding off,
an arrival so well foretold
by the setting forth the journey
will have seemed all along a return.

All questions will be answered.
Should the sense signal loss—
or, worse, disaster—even so,
at the sound of the last cadence,

when the long rhythms of the telling
lapse in a great easing fall
that finishes the whole,
prepare for a lift of startling fullness.

Let the speaking word ebb as it will
at the close, not hurried or slowed.
You'll feel the rightness of silence
and space.

NOTES

"The Need for Echoes" — Two literary antecedents sound here, the second more remotely: Theseus's "The lunatic, the lover, and the poet . . . ," at the beginning of act 5 of *A Midsummer Night's Dream,* and E. M. Forster's *A Passage to India* and its terrible echoing caves ("buom").

"Fred's Girl" — Apollo, the sun god, is also head of the Muses. In George Balanchine's ballet "Apollon Musagète" ("Apollo, Master of the Muses"), Apollo teaches Terpsichore how to dance. This master-Muse relationship informs many of Astaire's duets, especially in his earlier film work; his partnerships with Ginger Rogers, both Joan Leslie and Joan Fontaine, Rita Hayworth, and Paulette Goddard belong mainly to this period. The immediate inspiration for this poem was Astaire's wonderful master-Muse duet with Goddard in *Second Chorus* (1940). Irving Berlin's "Cheek to Cheek," for Astaire and Rogers's *Top Hat* (1935), begins, memorably, "Heaven, I'm in heaven / And my heart beats so that I can hardly speak . . . ," on its rising musical phrase.

"Poplar" — The language is, at first, nineteenth-century English-romantic, perhaps fulsomely so (I reach for Keats); then comes the plainly analytic language through which we moderns must interpret nature now. Wordsworth sees daffodils "Fluttering and dancing in the breeze," and later remembers their delightful "show." The spectator here experiences a double vision.

"Reading the Fall" — The waterfall described is beside a road that climbs Mount Rainier. The two closing stanzas refer to (in this order) *The Sound and the Fury, Death of a Salesman,* Elizabeth Bishop's "The Bight," *A Streetcar Named Desire, A Passage to India,* and *The Great Gatsby;* the previous stanza begins with an allusion to Proust's *petite phrase.* The poem's dedicatees are the superb advanced English students I taught at Lowell High School, in San Francisco. To them I owe my best reading skills.

"Song" — Originally called "Song of Myself," this poem is a kind of parody, though not a mocking one, of Walt Whitman's multiple, serial pantheistic identifications (in which Whitman is God, of course), the transformations occurring here at breathless, and I hope amusing, speed. The poem is not an earnest treatment of its subject, the act of writing poetry.

"Sunday Sorrow" — This poem began as a glib response to a friend's question, Why write poetry now? I wrote, in reply, "Beats live-in nurse / to nerves and joints / and Sunday sorrows." Later the notion of Sunday sorrow took on fuller life.

"Family Stories" — In chapter 6 of Edith Wharton's *The Custom of the Country,* this is said about Undine Spragg's mother: "Mrs. Spragg liked to repeat her stories. To do so gave her almost her sole sense of permanence among the shifting scenes of her life." In this poem, repeating a story is linked to a sense of permanence with a different value, and ultimately a different source.

"Through My Window" — The quotation from chapter 20 of *Middlemarch* is too long, and too good, to give in full in an epigraph: "If we had a keen vision and feeling of all ordinary human life, it would be like hearing the grass grow and the squirrel's heart beat, and we should die of that roar which lies on the other side of silence." The iambic pentameter of the poem's two central narratives lends them stature, but with a difference: the improvised mythical tale is, in manner, Classical-myth–telling pastiche, its anachronistic intrusions (such as "higher-powered") attempting lightness and humor, qualities of style characteristic of Ovid in particular. Having little time to spare on those "figures on a well-framed stage," I hope to evoke Pound's "Petals on a wet, black bough"—his stark, still figurative image of waiting passengers.

ACKNOWLEDGMENTS

I am grateful to the editors of the following journals, in which the poems named first appeared, some in a slightly different form.

Angle: "Sure Thing"

California Quarterly: "Sunday Sorrow"

Cider Press Review: "The Pigeon Is a Shoe" (included in the special print issue *Cider Press Review: Best of Volume 16*)

Cordite Poetry Review: "Finishing"

The MacGuffin: "The Need for Echoes" and "Orchestra, Advanced"

The Raintown Review: "Poplar"

Slant: "Fred's Girl," "Reading the Fall," and "Through My Window"

Tampa Review: "During Restless Sleep a Scene of Remarkable Stillness"

ABOUT THE AUTHOR

David Hathwell's poems have appeared in more than a dozen literary magazines, national and international, including *Tampa Review, The MacGuffin, Measure,* and the online journals *Cider Press Review, Driftwood Press,* and *Angle.* A former English teacher, he has degrees in English from Stanford University and Columbia University, as well as an advanced degree in music theory from Queens College of the City University of New York. He is now a piano student at the San Francisco Conservatory of Music and a bass in the Lesbian/Gay Chorus of San Francisco. ("My musical training, as much as any other influence, has shaped the character of my poetry.") He lives in San Francisco with Stephen Goldston, his partner of forty years and husband of seven. *Muses* is his debut collection.

Made in the USA
Charleston, SC
24 August 2016